Pebble™ Plus

Mighty Machines
Earthmovers

by Linda D. Williams

Consulting Editor: Gail Saunders-Smith, PhD

Consultant: Debra Hilmerson, Member
American Society of Safety Engineers
Des Plaines, Illinois

Capstone press

Mankato, Minnesota

Pebble Plus is published by Capstone Press,
151 Good Counsel Drive, P.O. Box 669, Mankato, Minnesota 56002.
www.capstonepress.com

1 2 3 4 5 6 09 08 07 06 05 04

Library of Congress Cataloging-in-Publication Data
Williams, Linda D.
    Earthmovers / by Linda D. Williams.
    p. cm.—(Pebble plus: mighty machines)
    Includes bibliographical refererences and index.
    ISBN 0-7368-2597-5 (hardcover)
    ISBN 0-7368-5135-6 (paperback)
    1. Earthmoving machinery—Juvenile literature. [1. Earthmoving machinery.]
I. Title. II. Series.
TA725.W38 2005
629.225—dc22   2003025767

Summary: Simple text and photographs present different kinds of earthmovers.

Editorial Credits
Martha E. H. Rustad, editor; Molly Nei, designer; Scott Thoms, photo researcher;
    Karen Hieb, product planning editor

Photo Credits
Bruce Coleman Inc./Cameron Davidson, 4–5; George H. Harrison, 12–13
Capstone Press Archive, 8–9, 18–19
constructionphotography.com, cover, 16–17, 20–21
Corbis/Roger Ressmeyer, 14–15
David R. Frazier Photolibrary, 6–7, 10–11
Steven J. Meunier, 1

Note to Parents and Teachers

The Mighty Machines series supports national standards related to science, technology, and society. This book describes and illustrates earthmovers. The images support early readers in understanding the text. The repetition of words and phrases helps early readers learn new words. This book also introduces early readers to subject-specific vocabulary words, which are defined in the Glossary section. Early readers may need assistance to read some words and to use the Table of Contents, Glossary, Read More, Internet Sites, and Index/Word List sections of the book.

Word Count: 121
Early-Intervention Level: 13

Table of Contents

Earthmovers 4

Kinds of Earthmovers 8

Mighty Machines 20

Glossary 22

Read More 23

Internet Sites 23

Index/Word List. 24

Earthmovers

Earthmovers dig, push,
pile, and lift. Earthmovers
do many jobs.

Earthmovers build roads
and runways. Earthmovers
work at building sites
and in mines.

Kinds of Earthmovers

Bulldozers are earthmovers
that push dirt and rocks.
Bulldozers move slowly on
rolling tracks.

track

Bulldozers make land flat for roads. Bulldozers smooth the land with steel blades.

blade

Backhoes are earthmovers that dig deep into the ground. Backhoes have digging arms with buckets.

bucket

Backhoes scoop up dirt
and lift it high in the air.
They pile the dirt into
dump trucks.

15

Dump trucks are earthmovers
that haul heavy loads.
Dump trucks move
on strong tires.

tire

The beds of dump trucks
tip up. Loads of dirt and
rocks fall onto the ground.

bed

Mighty Machines

Earthmovers work hard
together. Earthmovers
are mighty machines.

Glossary

blade—a wide, curved metal scoop in front of a bulldozer used to push, dig, or lift rocks and dirt

bucket—a scoop on a backhoe; a bucket is on the end of an arm.

building site—a place where something new is being made or constructed

mine—a place where workers dig up minerals that are underground

track—a wide metal belt that runs along the ground; a bulldozer has two tracks to help it move on rough ground.